Contents

Foreword
by Steve Davies

A very big welcome to the National Railway Museum, the world's largest and busiest railway museum, dedicated to connecting generations through the wonderful stories of railways and how they shape our world. We are a museum that enables people to explore the story of railways and of how they fit into that story. Through life enhancing experiences, we aim to allow you, our valued visitor, to gain greater appreciation of railways as a form of transport through an exciting, educational and memorable series of galleries, interactive and learning experiences.

The modern railway saw its origins in the United Kingdom, and its rapid development throughout the 19th and 20th Centuries, both at home and overseas, utterly transformed the daily lives of millions of people. Railways helped accelerate the pace of technological development in a broad number of fields thus directly and indirectly improving the prosperity, wealth and happiness of people across the globe. They also facilitated a major improvement in the way people spent their leisure time through greater access to, for example, coastal destinations, which themselves in turn developed into major tourist attractions. The railway also had a profound effect on the social cohesion of societies, and even influenced our diet – the innovation of fish and chips as a staple of the British diet being a classic example. They also enabled war to be fought more efficiently and on an industrial scale, with grave consequences for casualty numbers. More positively, the railway has for nearly 200 years been at the heart of our lives, associated with happiness, sadness, leisure, holidays, and work – and much more. And they continue to deliver an environmentally effective transport solution today, and into the future.

The Museum's collections range from the most powerful of steam locomotives, through to the most ornate carriages. They include models, archive material, photographic images, film and works of fine art. Compare the humble carriages used to transport passengers in the early 19th Century with the sheer splendour of our Royal Trains. Marvel at the beauty of the world's fastest steam locomotive Mallard. And get up close to the humble but essential freight locomotives which literally fuelled the industrial revolution and fed the nation. But most of all enjoy an amazing day out at the World's greatest railway museum.

Steve Davies MBE
Director, National Railway Museum

The National Railway Museum is the largest railway museum in the world.
Here you can learn all you ever wanted to know about railways. Where they
came from, how they work – and where they're going.

History of the NRM
The largest in the world

04 – 05

There has been a railway museum in York for over 80 years. The London & North
Eastern Railway set up its own collection of retired locomotives and other railway
paraphernalia back in 1925. Fifty years later, the present National Railway Museum
took its place.

It's much bigger than the original one because the planners had the brainwave of
converting an old steam engine shed. You can still see one of the turntables with all
the stub tracks off it where engines were serviced between turns of duty.

In 1990 the Museum expanded when an old goods depot was taken over and
converted. Since then more buildings have been added. Today there's even a link
to the live railway running just outside. And inside there's a collection of three million
items – everything from a Victorian uniform button to a high-speed Bullet Train.

Opposite page. The former engine shed that now houses the Great Hall, just before construction began in 1973.

This page top left. Watercolour by Edna Lumb showing the Weatherhill Winding Engine being installed in the Great Hall, 1975.

Top right. Engineering drawings on display in Search Engine, the museum's library and archive centre which opened in 2007.

Centre. The National Railway Museum's Oliver Cromwell hauling the Scarborough Spa excursion train, 2008.

Bottom. Locomotion, the National Railway Museum at Shildon, during construction. It opened its doors to visitors in 2004.

The Great Hall is the heart of the Museum. It used to be a locomotive shed known as York North. Everything today is bright, clean and airy. When it was a working shed it would have been the exact opposite: dirty and sooty, with puddles of water and things to trip over if you were not very careful.

Great Hall

06 – 07

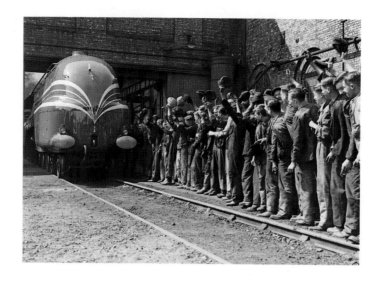

Few locomotives have had such a varied history as Duchess of Hamilton.

Duchess of Hamilton
Symbol of an era

08 – 09

Duchess of Hamilton was built in 1938, and its distinctive appearance was inspired by the streamlined design movement of the 1930s. The streamlining was also intended to compete with the London, Midland and Scottish Railway's rivals – the London and North Eastern Railway had launched their own streamlined 'Silver Jubilee' service in 1935.

Although striking to look at, the streamlined casing made it difficult to carry out repairs, and it was removed in 1947.

Duchess of Hamilton was withdrawn from service in 1964, after covering 1.5 million miles. The locomotive was bought by Billy Butlin and put on display at his Minehead holiday camp.

It finally became part of the National Collection in 1987, and after several years of operating on heritage railways, the engine returned to the workshops to be restreamlined. This work was completed in 2009, and Duchess of Hamilton is now restored to its stylish 1930s appearance.

NEW YORK WORLD'S FAIR
Distinguished Guest Train

In 1939 Duchess of Hamilton travelled to the New York World's Fair, where it took on the identity of another locomotive, 6220 Coronation. Duchess of Hamilton was a star attraction, and was seen by over 2 million people. The locomotive remained in America until 1942, when it returned home for service on Britain's wartime railways. For its new role in austerity Britain, the engine was repainted in plain black livery.

Opposite page. The first of LMS' streamlined locomotives, Coronation, leaves Crewe Works in 1937.

This page top left. In order to run on American railways, Duchess of Hamilton had to be fitted with a light and bell.

Top right. An advert for Duchess of Hamilton's appearance at the World's Fair, 1939.

Centre. Duchess of Hamilton on its return to the National Railway Museum, 2009.

Bottom. An unstreamlined Duchess of Hamilton hauls the Scarborough Spa excursion train in 1982.

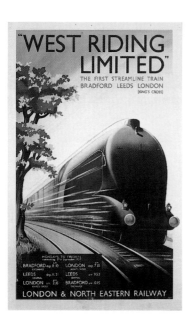

Mallard is the original flyer – it holds the title of fastest steam locomotive in the world. But is that world record really deserved?

Mallard
World beater

10 – 11

Mallard is a development of the Flying Scotsman design. Both were drawn up by the same man: Sir Nigel Gresley. Gresley did not want to design just a high-speed locomotive – he wanted an eye-catcher that would tempt more people to travel by train.

So he built a graceful, streamlined beauty with curves that caught everyone's attention. One day in 1938, Mallard was chosen for a secret attempt at the steam speed record. The man at the controls was driver Joe Duddington, and he took Mallard on a hell-for-leather dash down a long incline on the East Coast Main Line between Grantham and Peterborough.

A special recording carriage logged a top speed of 126mph. But it's almost certain that other steam locomotives travelled faster, particularly in the United States where fast running had to be kept secret because it was illegal!

Mallard is an A4 class, Pacific type locomotive. Pacific locomotives all shared the same type of wheels: four small carrying wheels under the cylinders at the front; six big driving wheels, all coupled together and another two carrying wheels under the cab. The A4 class was built to do one specific job: power light express trains at speed from London to Newcastle and Edinburgh. They excelled at it, cutting journey times and putting in some high-speed runs. The first four were turned out in a special silver and grey colour scheme to match the silver and grey carriages of the Silver Jubilee express.

Opposite page. LNER poster advertising the West Riding Limited service, 1938.

This page top. The designer of both Mallard and Flying Scotsman, Sir Nigel Gresley (1876–1941), pictured in the 1930s.

Main Picture. The fastest steam locomotive in the world, Mallard. The colour scheme – Garter Blue with bright red wheels – was devised to make the new streamlined locomotives stand out from the rest.

Bottom. Mallard, her crew and company officials pictured after her record-breaking run on 3 July, 1938.

Japan's high-speed railway revolution resulted in this remarkable machine – the forerunner of high-speed trains everywhere.

Shinkansen
The Bullet Train

12 – 13

It's hard to believe that the Bullet Train – or Shinkansen train to give it the correct Japanese name – was built in 1964, just four years after we had built the last British main line steam locomotive.

But it's true. The Japanese saw a big future for railways – but not in their traditional form. Instead, new trains on new railways would whisk passengers along at speeds of just over 130mph. The fastest in the world at the time, the Bullet Train used electric power and signals in the cab, not along the lineside, to operate safely, and had a punctuality record that was measured in seconds, not minutes.

The Japanese have built more generations of high-speed trains and this one, a Series 0, became obsolete. The Japanese Railway authorities agreed with Britain's National Railway Museum that one of their trains could have a permanent home here. So it was shipped over in an epic journey that became the subject of a TV documentary.

Opposite page. Publicity shot of the Shinkansen Train speeding past Mount Fuji, Japan. Courtesy Central Japan Railway Company.

This page top. *A series of Bullet Trains in Japan. Courtesy Central Japan Railway Company.*

Centre. *The Bullet Train rolls ashore in England during its epic journey from Japan to the National Railway Museum in York, May 2001.*

Bottom. *Shinkansen on display in the Museum.*

Series 0 Shinkansen trains were formed from fixed sets of carriages – rather like a British Intercity 125 train. They were designed to accelerate very quickly away from station stops and then cruise at full speed over long stretches of purpose-built, high-speed tracks which were maintained to a special high standard. The top speed of Shinkansen trains has been gradually increased until the fastest now operate at 199mph. One train set a Japanese speed record of 264mph. But the French – who followed the Japanese into high-speed trains – answered back with a TGV that set a world record of 320mph. Beat that!

Before it became a museum, the Great Hall was once a working railway building.

The Great Hall
Engine shed number four

14 – 15

Before it became a museum, the Great Hall was one of nine engine sheds in York. Built in 1877, the shed was used to house, clean and prepare steam locomotives for service. Heavy duty maintenance and repairs were carried out further afield, in locomotive works such as Darlington or Doncaster.

On 29 April 1942 the York sheds, along with York station, were badly damaged in a German air raid. Both sites were soon back in action after the raid, but one locomotive named Sir Ralph Wedgwood was completely destroyed.

Shed number four was used for working engines until 1967, and after the end of steam in 1968 was used to store redundant locomotives. When the National Railway Museum opened in 1975 the shed became known as the Great Hall.

The one remaining turntable was installed in 1954, and is 21.5 metres (70 feet) in diameter. It's powered by an electric motor, but early turntables were hand-operated. It sounds like a real slog for the crew, but if an engine is properly balanced – parked in just the right spot – it's remarkably easy to push a huge locomotive round by hand.

Opposite page. *Locomotives around the turntable in York motive power depot, about 1950.*

Centre. *Some of our locomotives gathered around the Great Hall turntable.*

Bottom. *The bomb-damaged locomotive Ralph Wedgewood before it was scrapped, 1942.*

Flying Scotsman is the locomotive that everyone has heard of. But why is this engine so well known? It's a long and intriguing story, which begins here…

Flying Scotsman

"THE FLYING SCOTSMAN"
FROM 1ST MAY
EDINBURGH
(WAVERLEY)
KING'S CROSS
WITHOUT STOP
392
MILES
CORRIDOR THROUGH TENDER
FRESH DRIVER AND FIREMAN
TAKE CONTROL WHILST
RUNNING
LNER
FRANK
NEWBOULD
PUBLISHED BY THE LONDON & NORTH EASTERN RAILWAY
HAYCOCK CADLE & GRAHAM LTD. LONDON E.C.4

Flying Scotsman is the best known locomotive in the world. But there was a train named Flying Scotsman too. Why are they both so famous?

Flying Scotsman
Our living legend

18 – 19   Flying Scotsman, the locomotive, was the third of a new type of express passenger locomotive built to work between London and Edinburgh. Her first brush with fame was at the British Empire Exhibition, staged at Wembley in 1924 and 1925, where she was seen by millions of people.

Then she became a film star in Britain's first 'talkie' – a film called 'The Flying Scotsman' – an adventure story based around a journey on the train. Soon after, she became the first locomotive to officially break the 100mph speed record on the trip from London to Leeds. The result: celebrity!

But a few years later, when newer locomotives came along, Scotsman was yesterday's news and led a more mundane existence until she was taken out of service in 1963 and prepared for the scrapheap.

Opposite page. Flying Scotsman's nameplate, 2004.

This page top. Flying Scotsman heads the Scarborough Express, 2004. Picture courtesy of The Press, York.

Bottom right. This is the train, but not the engine! The Flying Scotsman train arrives at Kings Cross Station some time in the 1930s. The locomotive is not Flying Scotsman, but No. 10000, an experimental design. Nigel Gresley is seen on the left, suggesting that this may have been a test run or even the inaugural run of the locomotive.

Flying Scotsman started life as an A1 class, Pacific type locomotive. She was modified several times to allow her to run faster and develop more power. The sloping sides of the wide firebox were designed to allow her to generate steam for long periods without the fire becoming clogged with ash. In the 1940s she was uprated to A3 class with a more powerful boiler. In British Railways days she was modified again, this time with a double chimney to make her generate more power. The A3 locomotives were seen by many enthusiasts – and professionals – as the kings of the tracks. Graceful, beautifully proportioned – but powerful too.

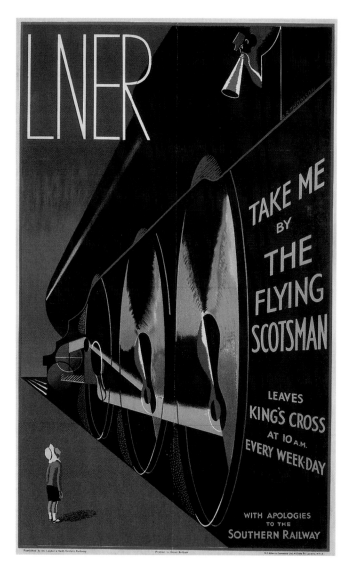

20 – 21   Just when it seemed that Flying Scotsman was doomed, a Doncaster businessman, Alan Pegler, stepped in and bought her outright. Scotsman had several other owners before finally becoming part of the National Collection in 2004. By that time the locomotive was 81 years old and had travelled almost 2.5 million miles.

The engine was completely dismantled and worn out parts were overhauled or replaced. Many of the original components remain, and when the restoration work is complete Flying Scotsman will be in as good condition as when it left Doncaster Works in 1923.

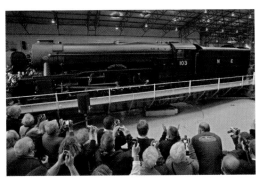

Long before the locomotive Flying Scotsman was built, there was a train using the same name running every day between Kings Cross Station, London and Edinburgh. No-one's quite sure when it actually became The Flying Scotsman – it had been known as The Scotch Express. The London & North Eastern Railway developed it as a prestige, luxury service. It was speeded up using more powerful locomotives – including Flying Scotsman herself. In 1928 it began running non-stop from London to Edinburgh.

Meanwhile, passengers enjoyed unrivalled luxury with a special three-carriage dining car set, a cocktail bar, a cinema – even a hairdresser!

Opposite page left. *LNER poster, 1932, part of a campaign to persuade travellers that the East Coast was a better route to Scotland than the rival West Coast line.*

Opposite page right. *The non-stop journey to Scotland took over eight hours so it could only be done by changing the footplate crew on the move. Special tenders with corridor connections were built and the reserve crew rode as passengers before using the gangway through the tender to take over just north of York. Here an engineman emerges from the passageway onto the footplate.*

This page top left. *Heavy engineering work on Flying Scotsman at Riley's & Son workshop.*

Top right. *Flying Scotsman's boiler and frame are lifted from the drive wheels.*

Bottom left. *Flying Scotsman in its wartime black livery, on the museum turntable, 2011.*

Bottom right. *The cab being prepared for repainting, 2011.*

Welcome to The Works where you can see how our engines are maintained, where we store the things we don't have room to show you properly and where you can learn about how trains are controlled.

The Works

The Warehouse is the Museum's cupboard – a storage space where we keep all the things we don't have room to display.

Warehouse
1,001 surprises

24 – 25

Most museums have stores – places where the things that there is just no room to put on show are kept safely. Instead of keeping them locked away we decided to throw ours open to the public!

Feel free to wander around and have a look at anything that catches your eye. The signalling equipment. The desk used by a famous railway company boss. Or the beautiful large-scale models of railway locomotives and carriages. There are thousands and thousands of things in here. There's bound to be something for you!

Opposite page. An 1849 sculpture of Britannia by John Thomas, from London's Euston Station, looks out across the Warehouse.

This page top. Over 8000 objects are stored in the Warehouse.

Bottom left. The Warehouse is home to hundreds of locomotive nameplates and workplates.

Bottom right. There are objects of every size in the Warehouse, from entire signal frames to cups and saucers.

Keeping a priceless collection in tip top condition is a labour of love!

Workshop Gallery
Step behind the scenes

26 – 27

The Workshop Gallery is a great way of seeing how the Museum's collection is maintained. You get the best view of what's going on, such as which locomotive is in for maintenance, and you can learn more about full-size railway workshops and what it was like to work in one.

Follow the gallery around and you'll reach the Working Railway area which tells you all about how trains are signalled and kept a safe distance apart from each other. There's a replica of an old-fashioned signalbox with levers and bells. And a link to the real railway just outside.

The screens show exactly what's happening in the computer-controlled signalling centre at York. See real trains moving along the displays – and then step out onto the balcony and see them for real!

When you've seen enough of what's happening in the Workshop, turn around and look at the display running along the gallery. It tells the story of the network of railway workshops that once provided almost everything that moved – and many things that didn't! There's also information about the workshops here in York which became famous for the quality of their carriages that operated all over the rail network.

Opposite page. *Workers building the underframes, or chassis, for a batch of new carriages, at the North Eastern Railway's carriage works in York in the early 1900s.*

This page top. *The Workshop Gallery allows visitors to see exactly what's going on.*

Bottom left. *The 1936 steam locomotive Green Arrow, under repair in the workshop.*

Bottom right. *Female cleaners cleaning wheels in No. 16 shop, Derby works, 1942.*

All kinds of things are restored, repaired and maintained in the Museum's own Workshop.

Workshop
We can fix it

28 – 29 Maintaining railway equipment is nothing like looking after your car. A range of specialist skills is needed. And steam locomotives need even more attention.

The Workshop is not large by railway standards, but it's capable of doing a lot. Many of the spare parts needed to keep things running aren't available off the shelf anymore. They have to be handmade and the Museum's small team of craftsmen know all about making something from nothing. You can see them at work from the gallery using skills that you may remember being taught at school – if you're old enough! Many of the craft skills such as metal and woodworking are rarely taught today.

The Museum is preserving these skills for future generations. It's a miniature version of the old railway workshops where thousands of people used to work. It could be a hard life with plenty of noise, dirt and petty regulations. You lost money if you were a minute late for work! But for many it was a secure job for life and sons followed their fathers – and grandfathers – into the railway works.

Railway workshops were a man's world. Most workers started from school and would spend up to seven years as apprentices, learning one of a dozen different trades from boilersmith to carriage upholsterer. Pay was nothing special, but you knew you were in a job for life with a clear career ladder to follow.

Women were noticeable by their absence – except during the two World Wars. Thousands of women stepped forward to take the places of men who went off to fight – only to have their jobs taken away when the men came back.

Opposite page. *Repairing Flying Scotsman's firebox.*

This page top. *Repainting Flying Scotsman's wheels in the museum's workshop, 2007.*

Bottom. *A 3' gauge locomotive, known as Handyman, undergoing repair work in 2008.*

The Station Hall might look like a small passenger station – but it's actually an old goods depot. In its heyday, this depot would have handled almost everything going in and out of York. Now it's one of the Museum's major display areas.

Station Hall

Railways were built to haul bulk freight rather than carry passengers.
But the idea caught on and changed the way we live and work forever.

Commuting
The 8.14 to town

32 – 33   Railways changed Britain in many ways. But one thing that no-one predicted when the first railways were being planned and built was the creation of the suburbs and the birth of the commuter.

Before railways, towns and cities had to be small, compact places. If you didn't own a horse and carriage, you walked to work. When railways came along, it dawned on land speculators and builders that you could cancel out distance with speed. It did not matter if you now lived miles away from the centre – it did not take any longer to get to and from work because trains were faster than walking.

Suburbia was created and the well-to-do began to move out to leafier areas with bigger houses and gardens. It also brought a new class system: First and Third Class, boldly painted on each carriage door. Commuting caught on in a big way, especially in London. Even today, 70 per cent of all rail journeys begin or end in London.

Opposite page. Commuters pass the departure board at Charing Cross station, 1970.

This page top. Workmen waiting at Liverpool Street Station, 1884.

Bottom. A 1931 poster advertising the Southern Railway's commuter services with fast electric trains.

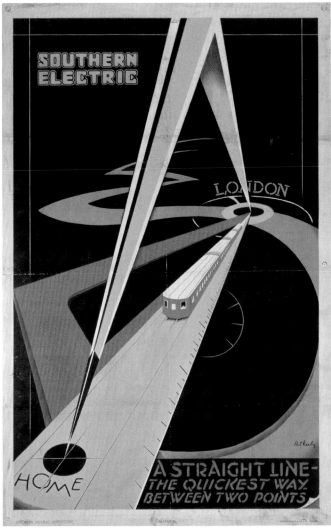

With commuter trains came the need to tell the time accurately everywhere in the country. Before rail travel, local areas had their own local time which could vary from London time by 15 or 20 minutes. That was useless for running a timetable, so, slowly but surely, the railway companies began imposing Standard (or 'Railway') Time on their networks. Look for the Regulator Clock to see how they did it. This one (right) came from Euston and guards' watches would be set by it. As they travelled over the line to Birmingham, they would take 'standard time' to each individual station. Finally, in 1880, time across the whole of Britain was standardised by Act of Parliament.

The rail network was built to carry heavy and bulky commodities like coal to fuel Britain's industrial revolution.

Freight
Eggs to elephants

34 – 35

The first railway builders saw their railways as a sort of conveyor belt for industrial production. Coal and minerals could suddenly be moved around the country quickly and cheaply. It helped establish steam power in thousands of factories which could then turn out mass-produced goods which the same railways carried to market.

As this process developed, railways became more and more useful and, in the age of steam, they carried virtually everything, fuelling not just industry but consumer society too. Freight also meant jobs, and when Station Hall was a goods depot it would have created hundreds of jobs: clerks to carters and everything in between.

Look out for the milk tank wagon and the special van that ripened bananas as they travelled to the shops. It's said that railways carried everything from eggs to circus elephants!

Opposite page. Station Hall in 1961, when it was still a working goods depot.

This page top. A railwayman sorts Christmas parcels at Waterloo Station, 1936.

Centre left. Unloading fresh strawberries from refrigerated vans, Manchester, 1936.

Centre right. Poster from 1933, advertising the London and North Eastern Railway's freight services.

Bottom. Marylebone Goods depot, around 1911.

"DOG TOOTH" LOADING DOCK, ARDWICK EAST GOODS DEPOT MANCHESTER

CAPACITY-MOBILITY ON THE L·N·E·R

ASK AT ANY L·N·E·R GOODS DEPOT FOR NEW BOOKLET "HOW THE L·N·E·R "EXPRESSES" FREIGHT"

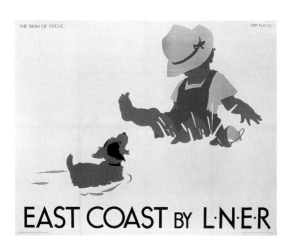

These days going on holiday usually means travelling by car or plane. But there was a time when almost everyone took their summer break by rail.

Holidays
Off to the seaside!

36 – 37 Excursion trains are an idea that's almost as old as railways themselves. The Liverpool & Manchester Railway – where Stephenson's Rocket made its name – ran its first excursion train just weeks after the opening ceremony in 1831, carrying 150 Sunday School members at a bargain fare.

The idea caught on, and as working lives improved, ordinary people began to use trains to have first days out, then weekends and, later still, their annual holiday. A vast network of trains sprang up that ran only on summer Saturdays, linking industrial towns and cities with seaside resorts to take people to and from their summer break.

Some of these trains still run today to places such as Newquay and Paignton. Day excursion trains carried millions to special events like race meetings and big football matches.

Blackpool boomed after the railways first arrived in 1846. The town was a popular destination for mill workers from Lancashire and West Yorkshire, and in its heyday attracted 17 million visitors a year. Alongside growing numbers of visitors, the town grew from a population of 500 in 1801 to 47,000 in 1901. Many of these new inhabitants set up hotels, shops or amusements for visitors. In 1895 a town official surveyed the stalls on the sea front – holidaymakers could choose to be entertained by 24 ventriloquists, 5 conjurors and even 1 chiropodist, who sold tickets to watch him cutting off corns.

Opposite page. Advertising poster, London & North East Railway, c. 1935.

This page top. Passengers boarding a train for Blackpool at Manchester Victoria station, August 1927.

Centre. Passengers arriving at Filey Holiday Camp station in 1950.

Bottom left. London, Midland and Scottish Railway poster advertising the North Wales resort of Rhyl, about 1935.

Bottom right. Midland Railway poster of about 1893, showing Blackpool seafront before the Tower was built.

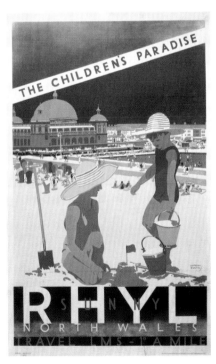

The Royal Family has been taking the train since 1842. They started a trend that's lasted until the present day.

Royal carriages
Travelling the realm

The first Royal trains were built by the private railway companies who were desperate to get the Royal seal of approval. It came on 13th June 1842 when Queen Victoria allowed the Great Western Railway to carry her from Windsor to London. She told the world she'd been 'quite charmed' by the experience.

From that moment, the race was on to provide the best and most lavish Royal carriages. The Royal Family has been travelling by train ever since – for everything from state occasions to morale-boosting wartime visits. You can still see a Royal Train out on the main line railway today.

The Royal Train has changed many times as old carriages became outdated. King Edward VII had a completely new train built in 1903. Another new carriage was added in 1941, and today the Royal Family travel in a train of air-conditioned coaches hauled by one of the latest diesel locomotives. For some members of the Royal Family, the train is still a favourite way of getting around. The Royal Train always carried four head lamps – the only train that was allowed to do so, so it would be instantly recognised by signalmen and other railway staff.

Opposite page. Queen Elizabeth II shakes hands with stationmaster, Mr Onyons, at Liverpool St Station, 1963.

This page top. King Edward VII and Queen Alexandra arriving at Newcastle Central Station, September 1906.

Middle. A lamp carried by locomotives hauling the Royal Train.

Bottom left. Queen Elizabeth II and the Duke of Edinburgh on board the Royal Train as it leaves Sunderland station, 1954.

Bottom right. King Edward VII saloon.

Queen Victoria rarely did things by halves. When she decided she needed a bigger and better carriage, she gave it her personal attention!

Queen Victoria's saloon
A palace on wheels

40 – 41   This carriage was Queen Victoria's personal saloon. It was built by the London & North Western Railway in 1869 after the Queen grumbled about the state of the old Royal coach. She chose the furniture, textiles and carpeting.

The carriage is a sort of time capsule, giving a rare glimpse of the very top of Victorian society. The complete train allowed the Queen to tour the country, with everything she needed for eating and sleeping – and room for her servants too.

But it was not built to last forever and that's why the Museum, aided by the Heritage Lottery Fund, has carried out a major conservation programme to preserve it for future generations.

The complete Royal Train cost £1,800 – a hefty sum back in 1869 when working families would exist on a few shillings a week. The Queen provided £800 of the cost. Floors were double thickness and packed with cork to reduce the noise when on the move. That's also the reason for the padding on the walls and ceilings. The two carriages – Day Saloon and Night Saloon – were originally separate, but they were rebuilt onto one long underframe in 1895, creating the vehicle you see today.

Opposite page. Queen Victoria, 1892.

This page top. The interior of Queen Victoria's saloon carriage.

Centre. Queen Victoria at Gosport Station, 1844. The carriage was one of the pair – the Day Saloon and the Night Saloon – which formed the first Royal Train.

Bottom. Two views of conservation work on Queen Victoria's carriage at the Museum, 2004.

To see railways in action, head to our outside space.

South Yard
The great outdoors

42 – 43

The South Yard is the Museum's outdoor area, and is home to our operating locomotives and railway lines. Steam rides, which run during school holidays, provide the perfect opportunity to get up close to working steam locomotives.

Stars of our collection often haul these rides, but we also play host to visiting locomotives such as Hogwarts Castle, the star of the Harry Potter films. When they're not working on these rides, or on loan to other heritage railways around the country, our working locomotives are stored and maintained in The Depot.

The South Yard is also home to our miniature railway. The locomotives that run on the railway are all driven by some of the museum's 300 volunteers.

Our working replica of Rocket is the only one in the world. It was built in 1979 to commemorate the 150th anniversary of the Rainhill Trials. The trials were organised by the Liverpool and Manchester Railway, who wanted to find the right locomotive for their line. Rocket was the winner, and earned the Stephensons £500 and a contract to supply the company's locomotives. The working replica was restored in 2010, and is often used to haul our steam rides.

Miniature Railway
The Museum's miniature railway might be small – but it's always a big draw with visitors. The miniature railway operates on 7¼" gauge tracks – a standard size for model engineers. It opened in 1997 and runs through a garden based on a scaled-down version of the English landscape which was designed by students of Bishop Burton College, just a few miles away from York. You are taken on a journey from the city to a wayside country platform. Trains are hauled by two petrol-engined locomotives. The tracks were laid and are still maintained by volunteers and the locomotives are driven entirely by volunteers. If you'd like to join them, they'd be pleased to see you.

Opposite page. The view from the footplate of a locomotive in the South Yard.

This page top. The working replica Rocket hauls a third class carriage.

Bottom left. Visitors ready to depart for a ride on the miniature railway.

Bottom right. Younger visitors can let off steam in our play area.

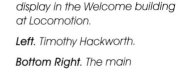

Timothy Hackworth

Top. Sans Pareil, built in 1829, on display in the Welcome building at Locomotion.

Left. Timothy Hackworth.

Bottom Right. The main Collection building, during Locomotion's annual Steam Gala.

Shildon has a long association with the railways

Locomotion
The National Railway Museum at Shildon

44

When the National Railway Museum decided to build another museum, Shildon was an obvious choice for location. The first steam hauled passenger train on a public railway departed from the town on 27 September 1825. This journey was made on the Stockton and Darlington Railway (S&DR).

The S&DR also opened its locomotive works in the town, known as Soho Works. In 1863 production moved to nearby Darlington, but Shildon went on to become Britain's largest wagon works. The works closed in 1984, but 20 years later, Locomotion opened, bringing together a number of historical sites and a brand new purpose-built museum. Locomotion houses more than 70 vehicles and is also home to over 40 special events a year.

Shildon was also home to Timothy Hackworth, the S&DR's resident engineer. Hackworth moved to Shildon in 1825, and over the next 25 years designed and built several pioneering locomotives. These included Sans Pareil, which competed in the Rainhill Trails. To find out more about him and his work in Shildon you can visit the cottage where he and his family lived.